ALASKA TRAVE

Alaska Travel Guide: Explore Majestic
Landscapes, Adventure Activities, and
Essential Travel Tips

Michael Keenan

All rights reserved. No part of this publication may be reproduced, distributed, or transmitted in any form or by any means, including photocopying, recording, or other electronic or mechanical methods, without the prior written permission of the publisher, except in the case of brief quotations embodied in critical reviews and certain other non-commercial uses permitted by copyright law.

Copyright © Michael Keenan.

Chapter 1: Discovering Alaska............3
Welcome to the Last Frontier: Introduction to Alaska's mystique and allure........................4
Geographical Marvels: Overview of Alaska's vast landscapes, from towering mountains to pristine coastlines............................6
Cultural Riches: Insight into the Deep Heritage of Indigenous Cultures and Modern Communities........................ 9

Chapter 2: Trip Planning Essentials..............13
Best Time to Visit: Seasonal highlights and what to expect throughout the year...............19
Month to month weather in Alaska and suitable activities............................23
Preparation Checklist: Must Have items for your Alaskan adventure........................29
Travel Costs and Budgeting: Detailed breakdown of expenses and moneysaving tips. 32

Chapter 3: Arriving and Getting Around.... 36
Major Entry Points: Key airports, seaports,

and border crossings.................................. 47
Transportation Choices: Navigating Alaska by air, sea, and land.................................. 52
Iconic Road Trips: Scenic drives and itineraries for road trippers........................ 57

Chapter 4: Cities and Towns...................... 63
Anchorage: Urban charm meets wilderness.... 64
Juneau: Capital city with a small town feel. 67
Fairbanks: Gateway to the Arctic and northern lights..70
Smaller Gems: Highlighting quaint towns and hidden villages..73

Chapter 5: Nature and Wildlife......................78
National Parks and Preserves: Exploring Denali, Glacier Bay, and more......................79
Wildlife Encounters: Where to see bears, eagles, whales, and other iconic species........ 86
Outdoor Activities: Hiking, kayaking, and adventure sports in the wild.......................... 90

Chapter 6: Unique Alaskan Experiences......96
Glacier Adventures: Cruise, hike, and fly

over stunning ice formations............................ 97
Dog Sledding: Embrace the spirit of the
Iditarod.. 102
Aurora Borealis: Best practices for chasing
the northern lights.. 107

Chapter 7: Historical and Cultural Sites..... 110
Native Heritage: Visiting cultural centers and
learning about indigenous history................ 110
Gold Rush Legacy: Tracing the steps of
fortune seekers..111
Museums and Historic Landmarks:
Preserving Alaska's storied past....................113

Chapter 8: Culinary Delights........................115
Local Flavors: Signature dishes and regional
specialties... 116
Dining Recommendations: From gourmet
restaurants to cozy diners............................. 119
Brewery and Distillery Tours: Tasting the best
of Alaska's craft beers and spirits................ 121

Chapter 9: Accommodation Options........... 125
Luxury Lodges and Resorts: Indulgent stays
in breathtaking settings.................................126

MidRange Hotels and Inns: Comfort and convenience for every traveler.......................129

Chapter 10: Travel Tips and Safety............131
Weather and Safety Precautions: Staying safe in diverse climates and terrains...................135
Respecting Wildlife and Nature: Guidelines for responsible tourism................................. 138
Emergency Contacts and Resources: Essential information for peace of mind.....139
Final thoughts... 143

Chapter 1: Discovering Alaska

Alaska, known as "The Last Frontier," is a land of breathtaking landscapes and rich culture. From its towering mountains and sprawling glaciers to the unique charm of its towns and the warmth of its people, Alaska offers an experience like no other. Whether you're fascinated by the history of the Gold Rush, eager to witness the mesmerizing northern lights, or simply looking to immerse yourself in the great outdoors, Alaska has something for every traveler. In this guide, we'll explore the best that Alaska has to offer, helping you plan an unforgettable adventure. Welcome to Alaska – let's start your journey!

Welcome to the Last Frontier: Introduction to Alaska's mystique and allure.

Alaska, often called "The Last Frontier," is a place like no other. This vast state is home to some of the most awe inspiring natural wonders on the planet. Imagine towering mountains, sprawling glaciers, and endless forests teeming with wildlife. Alaska's unique charm lies in its untouched beauty and the sense of adventure it offers. Whether you're watching grizzly bears fish for salmon in pristine rivers, cruising past glaciers that shimmer in the sunlight, or marveling at the northern lights dancing across the sky, Alaska never fails to captivate.

But Alaska is more than just stunning scenery. It's a land rich in culture and history. Indigenous communities have called this place home for thousands of years, and their traditions and stories add depth to the Alaskan experience. From the bustling city of Anchorage to the quaint charm of smaller towns like Talkeetna and Skagway, each part of Alaska offers its own slice of local flavor.

As you explore Alaska, you'll find that its mystique comes from the blend of rugged wilderness and vibrant culture. It's a place where adventure awaits around every corner, inviting you to discover its many wonders.

Geographical Marvels: Overview of Alaska's vast landscapes, from towering mountains to pristine coastlines.

Alaska's geographical diversity is nothing short of extraordinary, offering a stunning array of landscapes that captivate the imagination. From the rugged peaks of the Alaska Range to the serene beauty of its vast coastlines, this state is a paradise for nature lovers and adventure seekers alike.

❖ **The Majestic Mountains**

One of Alaska's most iconic features is its towering mountains. The Alaska Range, home to Denali (formerly known as Mount McKinley), North America's highest peak, is a dramatic sight. These mountains are not just tall but also incredibly scenic, with snowcapped peaks that pierce the sky and provide a backdrop for countless outdoor activities. Whether you're hiking through alpine meadows, skiing down pristine slopes, or simply enjoying the view from a distance, Alaska's mountains are truly aweinspiring.

❖ **Glaciers and IceFields**

Alaska boasts more glaciers than any other state in the U.S., with over 100,000 of these icy giants. Glaciers such as Mendenhall and Hubbard are accessible to visitors and offer a glimpse into the powerful forces of nature. These glaciers carve through valleys, creating spectacular landscapes and feeding into vibrant ecosystems. Glacier Bay National Park is a mustvisit, where you can witness massive glaciers calving into the sea, creating thunderous splashes and floating icebergs.

❖ **Pristine Coastlines**

The coastline of Alaska stretches for more than 6,600 miles, more than all other U.S. states combined. This extensive shoreline is dotted with fjords, bays, and inlets, each with its own unique charm. The Inside Passage, a coastal route through a network of islands and waterways, offers some of the most scenic marine landscapes in the world. Wildlife thrives here, with humpback whales, orcas, sea lions, and puffins frequently spotted. The coastline is also home to charming coastal towns and fishing villages where you can experience local culture and cuisine.

❖ **Lush Forests and Tundra**

Alaska's forests are vast and varied, from the temperate rainforests of the Southeast to the boreal forests further north. These forests are rich in biodiversity, providing habitats for a wide array of wildlife, including bears, moose, and wolves. As you travel further north, the landscape transitions to tundra, a unique ecosystem characterized by its hardy vegetation and permafrost. The tundra blooms with wildflowers in the summer, creating a colorful and resilient landscape.

❖ **Rivers and Lakes**

The state is crisscrossed by numerous rivers and dotted with countless lakes, adding to its geographical diversity. The Yukon River, one of the longest rivers in North America, winds its way through Alaska, offering opportunities for boating, fishing, and wildlife viewing. The lakes, from the massive Iliamna to the countless smaller ones, provide serene spots for kayaking, fishing, and simply soaking in the natural beauty.

Alaska's geographical marvels are a testament to the raw, untamed beauty of nature. Each landscape, whether it's the towering mountains, expansive glaciers, pristine coastlines, lush forests, or tranquil waters, tells a story of natural wonder and invites visitors to explore and be awed.

Cultural Riches: Insight into the Deep Heritage of Indigenous Cultures and Modern Communities

❖ **Indigenous Cultures**

Historical Background

Indigenous cultures are those that have been present in a region for millennia, often predating colonial and modern influences. These cultures typically have a deep connection to their land, which shapes their traditions, languages, and social structures.

❖ **Art and Craft**

Indigenous art is renowned for its intricate designs and symbolic meanings. For instance, Native American tribes such as the Navajo and Hopi are known for their weaving and pottery, which often include traditional patterns and symbols representing aspects of their spirituality and worldview.

❖ **Traditional Practices**

Many indigenous communities practice traditional ceremonies and rituals that are central to their identity. Examples include the Sundance Ceremony of the Lakota people or the Potlatch ceremonies of the Pacific Northwest tribes. These rituals often involve storytelling, dance, music, and communal feasting.

❖ **Languages**

Indigenous languages are crucial to cultural preservation, embodying unique worldviews and knowledge systems. Many of these languages are endangered, with efforts being made to revitalize and teach them to younger generations.

- ❖ **Knowledge and Wisdom**

    Traditional ecological knowledge, passed down through generations, offers valuable insights into sustainable living and environmental stewardship. Indigenous practices often include methods of farming, hunting, and land management that are adapted to local ecosystems.

Modern Communities

Cultural Integration

Modern communities often blend traditional practices with contemporary lifestyles. This integration can be seen in how indigenous art is adapted for modern contexts or how traditional ceremonies are celebrated alongside national holidays.

Revitalization Efforts

There is a growing movement to revitalize and preserve indigenous cultures through education, media, and community initiatives. Programs aimed at teaching indigenous languages in schools or promoting indigenous artists and authors help keep cultural heritage alive.

Economic Development
Indigenous communities are increasingly involved in economic activities, including tourism, which can provide a source of income while also promoting cultural exchange. Many communities operate cultural centers, craft markets, and guided tours that offer visitors insights into their heritage.

Social and Political Advocacy
Modern indigenous communities are active in advocating for their rights and sovereignty. This includes efforts to secure land rights, protect sacred sites, and ensure representation in political and social arenas.

In summary, exploring the deep heritage of indigenous cultures provides a window into diverse ways of life that have evolved over centuries. At the same time, understanding modern communities highlights the dynamic nature of cultural preservation and adaptation in the contemporary world.

Chapter 2: Trip Planning Essentials

Research and Information Gathering

Destination Research: Alaska is vast with diverse landscapes ranging from icy glaciers to dense forests. Focus your research on the specific regions you plan to visit, such as Anchorage, Denali National Park, the Kenai Peninsula, or the Inside Passage. Learn about the climate, key attractions, and local culture.

Local Customs and Etiquette: Alaska is known for its friendly and welcoming communities. Familiarize yourself with local customs, especially if visiting indigenous communities. Respect the environment and wildlife, following the Leave No Trace principles.

☐ **Budgeting**

Cost Estimation: Alaska can be an expensive destination, particularly in peak travel seasons. Budget for transportation (including flights, ferries, and possibly rental cars), accommodation, meals, activities (such as guided tours, fishing trips, and park entry fees), and gear rental.

Currency and Exchange Rates: The U.S. dollar is the currency used in Alaska. Ensure you have enough cash for remote areas where card payments might not be accepted. Consider the costs of any additional activities or excursions you might spontaneously decide to take.

☐ **Itinerary Planning**

MustSee Attractions: Prioritize key attractions such as Denali National Park, Kenai Fjords National Park, Glacier Bay, and the northern lights. Plan for outdoor activities like hiking, kayaking, wildlife viewing, and glacier tours.

Logistics: Given Alaska's size, plan your logistics carefully. Distances between destinations can be vast, and some areas are only accessible by plane or boat. Allow ample travel time and consider weather related delays.

☐ **Accommodation**

Types of Accommodation: Options range from luxury lodges and hotels to budgetfriendly hostels, campgrounds, and RV parks. Book well in advance, especially during the peak summer season.

Location and Amenities: Choose accommodations based on proximity to the activities and attractions you plan to visit.

Consider amenities such as shuttle services, guided tours, and onsite dining options.

☐ **Transportation**

Modes of Transport: Flights are common for long distance travel within Alaska. Rental cars, ferries (via the Alaska Marine Highway), and small planes are popular for reaching remote areas. Plan for scenic drives on routes like the Seward Highway or Denali Highway.

Local Transportation: In towns and cities, local buses, taxis, and rideshares are available. Consider renting a car for flexibility, especially for exploring rural areas and national parks.

☐ **Travel Documents**

Passports and Visas: Ensure your passport is valid if you are an international traveler. U.S. citizens do not need a visa, but international visitors should check visa requirements.

Travel Insurance: Obtain comprehensive travel insurance that covers medical emergencies, trip cancellations, and outdoor activities. Alaska's remote areas can pose unique risks, making insurance essential.

☐ **Health and Safety**

Vaccinations and Health Precautions: No special vaccinations are required for Alaska, but ensure routine vaccinations are up to date. Pack a travel health kit with medications, insect repellent, and first aid supplies.

Safety Tips: Be prepared for wildlife encounters and follow safety guidelines for bears and moose. Stay informed about weather conditions and be prepared for sudden changes. Inform someone of your travel plans when exploring remote areas.

☐ **Packing**

Clothing and Essentials: Pack layers to accommodate varying weather conditions, including waterproof and windproof outerwear. Bring sturdy hiking boots, warm clothing, gloves, hats, and sunscreen. Don't forget binoculars for wildlife viewing.

Travel Light: Use packing cubes and compression bags to organize and save space. Pack essential gear for outdoor activities, such as hiking poles, a reusable water bottle, and a backpack.

☐ **Travel Apps and Tools**

Navigation and Maps: Download offline maps and navigation apps like Google Maps. Use apps like AllTrails for hiking trails and Aurora Forecast to track northern lights activity.

Travel Management: Utilize travel management apps like TripIt to keep track of your itinerary, reservations, and important documents. Apps like Weather Underground can provide detailed weather forecasts.

By addressing these essentials, you can ensure a well prepared and enjoyable trip to Alaska, allowing you to fully appreciate the natural beauty and unique experiences this remarkable destination offers.

Best Time to Visit: Seasonal highlights and what to expect throughout the year.

Spring (March to May)

Weather: Spring in Alaska sees gradually warming temperatures and increasing daylight. In March, temperatures can still be quite cold, but by May, daytime highs can reach the 50s to 60s °F (1015 °C).

Highlights:

Northern Lights: Early spring is still a good time to catch the northern lights, particularly in March.

Wildlife Viewing: Animals start to emerge from hibernation, and bird migrations begin. It's a good time to see moose, bears, and other wildlife.

Shoulder Season: Fewer tourists compared to summer, leading to lower prices and less crowded attractions.

Summer (June to August)

Weather: Summer is the warmest and busiest season, with temperatures ranging from 60s to

70s °F (1525 °C) in most areas. Coastal regions can be cooler.

Highlights:

Midnight Sun: The long daylight hours, especially around the summer solstice, provide ample time for outdoor activities. In the far north, the sun doesn't set for several weeks.

Outdoor Activities: Ideal for hiking, fishing, kayaking, wildlife viewing, and exploring national parks. Denali National Park and Kenai Fjords National Park are particularly popular.

Festivals: Summer hosts many local festivals, including the Alaska State Fair in Palmer and the Seward Silver Salmon Derby.

Cruises: Peak season for Alaska cruises, offering spectacular views of glaciers, fjords, and coastal wildlife.

Fall (September to November)

Weather: Fall sees cooling temperatures and shorter days. September can still be relatively mild, but by November, winter conditions start to set in.

Highlights:

Fall Foliage: Early fall brings beautiful autumn colors, especially in the interior and mountainous regions.

Northern Lights: The aurora borealis becomes more visible again as nights grow longer, particularly from midSeptember onward.

Wildlife: Animals like bears are actively feeding before winter hibernation, making for good wildlife viewing opportunities.

Lower Prices: Shoulder season rates for accommodation and tours as the summer crowds diminish.

Winter (December to February)

Weather: Winter in Alaska is cold, with temperatures often below freezing. Interior regions can experience extreme cold, while coastal areas tend to be milder.

Highlights:

Northern Lights: Winter offers some of the best opportunities to see the northern lights due to long, dark nights and clear skies.

Winter Sports: Ideal for skiing, snowboarding, snowshoeing, dog sledding, and ice fishing.

Popular destinations include Alyeska Resort and Fairbanks.

Festivals: Winter events like the Iditarod Trail Sled Dog Race and the World Ice Art Championships attract visitors.

Peaceful Scenery: Winter landscapes are serene and less crowded, offering a unique perspective on Alaska's natural beauty.

Seasonal Considerations

Crowds and Costs: Summer is the peak tourist season, leading to higher prices and crowded attractions. Booking accommodation and tours in advance is recommended. Spring and fall offer a good balance of mild weather and fewer tourists, while winter provides a quieter, more intimate experience with opportunities for winter activities and northern lights viewing.

Accessibility: Some remote areas and national parks are more accessible in summer due to better weather and open roads. Winter travel can be challenging due to snow and ice, requiring more preparation and possibly limiting access to certain regions.

Each season in Alaska offers distinct experiences, making it a year round destination depending on your interests and tolerance for varying weather conditions.

Month to month weather in Alaska and suitable activities

January
Weather: Very cold, with temperatures ranging from 20°F to 20°F (29°C to 6°C) in the interior and slightly warmer along the coast.
Activities:
　Northern lights viewing
　Dog sledding
　Snowmobiling
　Ice fishing
　Skiing and snowboarding at Alyeska Resort

February
Weather: Similar to January, with slightly longer days. Temperatures remain cold.
Activities:

Winter festivals, such as the Fur Rendezvous in Anchorage
Northern lights viewing
Cross Country skiing
Dog sledding

March

Weather: Still cold, but daylight increases. Temperatures range from 0°F to 30°F (18°C to 1°C).

Activities:
Iditarod Trail Sled Dog Race
Northern lights viewing
Winter sports, including skiing and snowshoeing
Wildlife spotting as animals start to emerge from hibernation

April

Weather: Transition month with milder temperatures, ranging from 20°F to 40°F (6°C to 4°C).

Activities:
Spring wildlife viewing

Northern lights viewing early in the month
Hiking lower elevation trails
Birdwatching during migration

May

Weather: Warming up, with temperatures ranging from 30°F to 55°F (1°C to 13°C). Snow begins to melt.

Activities:
Hiking and biking
Wildlife viewing, including bear watching
Fishing season starts
Visiting national parks as they open for the season

June

Weather: Summer begins, with temperatures ranging from 45°F to 65°F (7°C to 18°C). Long daylight hours.

Activities:
Hiking and camping
Fishing, especially for salmon

Kayaking and canoeing
Wildlife tours
Visiting Denali National Park

July

Weather: Warmest month, with temperatures ranging from 50°F to 70°F (10°C to 21°C).
Activities:
Hiking, camping, and backpacking
Glacier tours and cruises
Fishing and wildlife viewing
Attending local festivals and events
Whale watching

August

Weather: Warm but starting to cool slightly, with temperatures ranging from 45°F to 65°F (7°C to 18°C).
Activities:
Continuation of summer activities like hiking and fishing

Berry picking
Wildlife viewing, especially bears
Visiting Kenai Fjords National Park

September

Weather: Cooling down, with temperatures ranging from 35°F to 55°F (2°C to 13°C). Fall colors emerge.

Activities:
Fall foliage tours
Hiking and biking
Northern lights viewing begins again
Fishing and hunting
Wildlife viewing

October

Weather: Colder with early snowfall possible, temperatures ranging from 25°F to 40°F (4°C to 4°C).

Activities:
Northern lights viewing
Scenic drives to see fall foliage

Early winter sports in some areas
Visiting museums and cultural centers

November
Weather: Cold, with increasing snowfall. Temperatures range from 10°F to 30°F (12°C to 1°C).
Activities:
Northern lights viewing
Dog sledding and snowmobiling
Skiing and snowboarding preparations
Indoor activities like visiting local museums and galleries

December
Weather: Very cold, with long nights. Temperatures range from 0°F to 20°F (18°C to 6°C).
Activities:
Northern lights viewing
Winter festivals and holiday events

Skiing, snowboarding, and snowshoeing
Ice fishing and ice skating
Dog sledding

Preparation Checklist: Must Have items for your Alaskan adventure.

Clothing
Layered Clothing

Base Layer: Moisture wicking shirts and thermal underwear.

Mid Layer: Insulating layers such as fleece or down jackets.

Outer Layer: Waterproof and windproof jacket and pants.

Warm Accessories
Gloves or mittens
Warm hat (beanie or balaclava)
Scarf or neck gaiter

Footwear
Sturdy, waterproof hiking boots
Warm socks (wool or synthetic)

Comfortable shoes for casual wear
Other Clothing
Lightweight, quick dry clothing for summer
Swimsuit (for hot springs or indoor pools)

Gear and Equipment
Backpack: Durable and comfortable for day trips and hikes.
Water Bottle: Reusable and insulated to keep drinks hot or cold.
Hydration System: Optional for long hikes.
Binoculars: For wildlife and bird watching.
Camera: With extra batteries and memory cards.
Headlamp/Flashlight: With extra batteries, especially for winter months.
Sunglasses: UV protection and polarized lenses.
Sunscreen and Lip Balm: With SPF protection.
Insect Repellent: Particularly for summer trips.
First Aid Kit: Including bandages, antiseptic wipes, pain relievers, and personal medications.
Multi Tool or Knife: Useful for various tasks.

Camping and Outdoor Activities

Tent: Suitable for the season and conditions.

Sleeping Bag: Rated for the lowest expected temperatures.

Sleeping Pad: For insulation and comfort.

Cooking Gear: Portable stove, fuel, cookware, and utensils.

Food and Snacks: High Energy and easy to prepare options.

Fire Starter Kit: Waterproof matches, lighter, and fire starters.

Fishing Gear: If you plan to fish, including necessary permits.

Personal Items

Travel Documents: ID, passport (if needed), and any necessary permits.

Cash and Cards: Some remote areas may not accept credit cards.

Travel Insurance: Comprehensive coverage for health, cancellations, and activities.

Toiletries: Basic personal hygiene items in travel sized containers.

Towel: Quickdry travel towel.

Entertainment: Books, ereader, or other personal entertainment for downtime.

Seasonal Considerations

Winter: Additional warm layers, insulated boots, crampons or microspikes for icy conditions, and hand/foot warmers.

Summer: Lightweight clothing, rain gear, sunhat, and extra insect repellent.

By packing these essentials, you'll be well prepared for the diverse and often unpredictable conditions you'll encounter in Alaska, ensuring a safe and enjoyable adventure.

Travel Costs and Budgeting: Detailed breakdown of expenses and moneysaving tips.

Here's a detailed breakdown of expenses and money saving tips for traveling in Alaska:

Alaska Travel Costs and Budgeting

Transportation

Flights:

Cost: $300-$700 roundtrip from the continental US.

Tips: Book in advance, use fare comparison tools, and consider flying into Anchorage, which is usually cheaper than smaller airports.

Rental Cars:

Cost: $50- $150 per day.

Tips: Book early, look for discounts, and consider renting from local agencies. Check if your accommodation offers shuttle services to avoid rental for the entire stay.

Public Transportation:

Cost: Anchorage public buses $2 per ride or $5 for a day pass.

Tips: Use public transport where possible, especially in cities like Anchorage and Fairbanks.

Ferries:
Cost: $50-$300 depending on the route and length.
Tips: Book well in advance and consider the Alaska Marine Highway System for scenic travel and savings on longer routes.

Accommodation
Hotels:
Cost: $100 -$300 per night.
Tips: Book early, especially in peak season (JuneAugust). Consider staying in motels, lodges, or B&Bs for more affordable options.

Camping:
Cost: $15-$30 per night for campground fees.
Tips: Camping can save money and offer unique experiences. Look for free or lower cost public campgrounds and national parks.

Vacation Rentals:
Cost: $80 -$200 per night.
Tips: Great for groups or families. Check sites like Airbnb or Vrbo for deals.

Food and Drink
Restaurants:

Cost: $10-$30 per meal.

Tips: Look for local diners and food trucks for cheaper meals. Dining out in smaller towns tends to be less expensive than in touristheavy areas.

Groceries:

Cost: $50- $100 per week per person.

Tips: Shop at larger stores like Fred Meyer or Walmart for better prices. Consider preparing some meals if you have kitchen access.

Activities and Tours
National Parks:

Cost: $15-$30 for entry fees.

Tips: Purchase an annual pass if visiting multiple parks. Take advantage of free ranger led programs and activities.

Guided Tours:

Cost: $50 -$300 depending on the activity.

Tips: Book in advance, look for package deals, and consider self guided options for hiking and sightseeing.

Wildlife Excursions:
Cost: $100-$200 for whale watching, bear viewing, etc.

Tips: Combine tours for discounts. Research local tour companies for best prices.

By planning ahead and utilizing these tips, you can experience Alaska's breathtaking landscapes and unique culture without breaking the bank.

Chapter 3: Arriving and Getting Around

Arriving in Alaska
Major Airports:
Ted Stevens Anchorage International Airport (ANC):
The primary gateway for most travelers.

Offers numerous domestic flights and some international connections.

Fairbanks International Airport (FAI):

Serves as the main entry point for visitors to the interior and northern Alaska.

Fewer flights compared to Anchorage but still well connected.

Juneau International Airport (JNU):

Main access point for the southeastern part of the state.

Often requires a connection through Anchorage or Seattle.

Tips for Arriving:

Advance Booking: Secure your flights well in advance, especially for summer travel.

Flexible Dates: If possible, be flexible with your travel dates to find the best deals.

RedEye Flights: Consider redeye flights for potential savings.

Getting Around Alaska

Rental Cars:

Availability: Major rental companies operate in Anchorage, Fairbanks, and Juneau.

Cost: **$50-$150** per day.

Tips:

Book early to ensure availability and better rates.

Check for discounts and consider local rental agencies.

Alaska Railroad:

Routes: Connects Anchorage, Fairbanks, Seward, and other key destinations.

Cost: **$70-$200** depending on the route and class of service.

Tips:

Book in advance, especially for popular routes like Anchorage to Denali.

Consider multi day passes if planning extensive train travel.

Buses and Shuttles:

Public Buses: Available in larger cities like Anchorage and Fairbanks.

Cost: $2 per ride or $5 for a day pass.

Private Shuttles: Operate between major destinations.

Cost: Varies, typically $30-$100 depending on the route.

Tips:

Research shuttle schedules and book in advance during peak season.

Utilize public buses for cost effective travel within cities.

Ferries:

Alaska Marine Highway System (AMHS):

Connects coastal communities from the Aleutian Islands to Southeast Alaska.

Cost: **$50-$300** depending on the route and accommodation type.

Tips:

Book well in advance for popular routes.

Consider traveling by ferry for scenic and leisurely travel.

Domestic Flights:

Bush Planes: Essential for reaching remote areas not connected by road.

Cost: $100-$500 depending on distance and demand.

Tips:

Book with reputable airlines that specialize in bush flights.

Plan for potential weather related delays.

Navigating the Road System

Highways:

Major Routes: Alaska Highway (connects to Canada), Seward Highway (Anchorage to Seward), and Parks Highway (Anchorage to Fairbanks).

Conditions: Roads can be challenging due to weather and wildlife; always check conditions before travel.

Tips:

Ensure your rental car has adequate insurance and emergency supplies.

Drive during daylight hours for better visibility and safety.

Bicycles:

Rental Services: Available in Anchorage, Fairbanks, and popular tourist areas.

Cost: $20-$50 per day.

Tips:

Explore bike friendly trails and paths for a unique way to see the sights.

Wear appropriate gear and be cautious of wildlife and weather conditions.

By planning your transportation options carefully and considering the tips provided, you can navigate Alaska efficiently and enjoy the state's stunning landscapes and unique attractions.

Visa Types for Alaska Travel

Traveling to Alaska generally follows the same visa requirements as entering any other part of the United States. Here are the main types of visas and entry permits you might need, depending on your nationality and purpose of visit:

Visa Waiver Program (VWP)

Eligibility: Citizens of 40 participating countries, including most European countries, Australia, Japan, South Korea, and Singapore.

Requirements:

Must have an approved ESTA (Electronic System for Travel Authorization).

Stay is limited to 90 days for tourism, business, or transit purposes.

Must have a return or onward ticket.

Cost: $21 for the ESTA application.

Tips:

Apply for ESTA at least 72 hours before your flight.

Ensure your passport is valid for at least six months beyond your intended stay.

Tourist Visa (B2 Visa)

Eligibility: Required for travelers from countries not included in the Visa Waiver Program.

Requirements:

Complete the DS160 online application form.

Schedule and attend a visa interview at a U.S. embassy or consulate.

Provide proof of financial stability, ties to your home country, and intent to return.

Cost: $160 nonrefundable application fee.

Tips:

Apply well in advance, as the process can take several weeks.

Prepare for your interview with all required documentation and a clear explanation of your travel plans.

Business Visa (B1 Visa)

Eligibility: For travelers visiting Alaska for business purposes such as meetings, conferences, or contract negotiations.

Requirements:

Complete the DS160 online application form.

Schedule and attend a visa interview at a U.S. embassy or consulate.

Provide proof of business activities, financial stability, and intent to return.

Cost: $160 nonrefundable application fee.

Tips:

Provide detailed information about your business activities and purpose of visit.

Have supporting documents from your employer or business partners in the U.S.

Student Visa (F1 Visa)

Eligibility: For international students enrolled in an academic program in Alaska.

Requirements:

Acceptance into a U.S. educational institution.

Complete the DS160 online application form and the I20 form from your school.

Pay the SEVIS fee.

Schedule and attend a visa interview.

Cost: $160 visa application fee + $350 SEVIS fee.

Tips:

Start the application process early, as it can take several months.

Provide proof of enrollment, financial stability, and ties to your home country.

Exchange Visitor Visa (J1 Visa)

Eligibility: For individuals participating in an exchange program, including scholars, researchers, and teachers.

Requirements:

Acceptance into a U.S. Department of State approved exchange program.

Complete the DS160 online application form and the DS2019 form from your program sponsor.

Pay the SEVIS fee.

Schedule and attend a visa interview.

Cost: $160 visa application fee + **$220** SEVIS fee.

Tips:

Ensure your exchange program is approved by the U.S. Department of State.

Provide proof of your program participation, financial stability, and intent to return.

Work Visa (H1B, L1, O1, etc.)

Eligibility: For individuals employed by a U.S. company or organization.

Requirements:

Job offer from a U.S. employer who will sponsor your visa.

Complete the relevant application forms (e.g., DS160) and provide supporting documents.

Schedule and attend a visa interview.

Cost: Varies by visa type; generally **$190** for the application fee.

Tips:

Ensure your employer is familiar with the sponsorship process.

Provide detailed information about your job and qualifications.

Transit Visa (C Visa)

Eligibility: For travelers passing through the U.S. en route to another country.

Requirements:

Complete the DS160 online application form.

Schedule and attend a visa interview.

Provide proof of onward travel and valid visas for your destination country.

Cost: $160 nonrefundable application fee.

Tips:

Clearly explain the purpose of your transit and provide travel itinerary details.

Ensure all your travel documents are in order.

By understanding the visa requirements and preparing accordingly, you can ensure a smooth entry process for your trip to Alaska.

Major Entry Points: Key airports, seaports, and border crossings.

Key Airports

Ted Stevens Anchorage International Airport (ANC)

Location: Anchorage, the largest city in Alaska.

Importance: The main gateway for both domestic and international travelers.

Facilities:

Two terminals: North Terminal for international flights and South Terminal for domestic flights.

Numerous car rental agencies, restaurants, shops, and hotels nearby.

Tips:

Take advantage of free WiFi and convenient shuttle services to downtown Anchorage.

Consider staying in Anchorage for a night to adjust to any time differences.

Fairbanks International Airport (FAI)
Location: Fairbanks, in the interior of Alaska.
Importance: Serves as a crucial entry point for visitors heading to Denali National Park and the Arctic regions.
Facilities:
One terminal with various amenities including dining options and gift shops.
Car rentals and shuttle services available.
Tips:
Plan to visit local attractions such as the Chena Hot Springs or the University of Alaska Museum of the North.

Juneau International Airport (JNU)
Location: Juneau, the capital city of Alaska.
Importance: The main access point for Southeast Alaska and the Inside Passage.
Facilities:
Small terminal with basic amenities, including a café and gift shop.

Limited car rentals; taxis and shuttles are primary means of transport.

Tips:

Book flights early as Juneau is only accessible by plane or boat.

Explore local highlights such as Mendenhall Glacier and the Alaska State Capitol.

Key Seaports

Port of Anchorage

Location: Anchorage.

Importance: The busiest port in Alaska, handling a large portion of the state's goods.

Facilities:

Docking facilities for cargo ships, cruise ships, and ferries.

Close proximity to the city center and airport.

Port of Seward

Location: Seward, on the Kenai Peninsula.

Importance: A major hub for cruise ships and gateway to Kenai Fjords National Park.

Facilities:

Cruise ship terminals, cargo docks, and passenger facilities.

Close to Seward's city center, restaurants, and accommodations.

Port of Juneau

Location: Juneau.

Importance: A popular stop for cruise ships exploring the Inside Passage.

Facilities:

Multiple cruise ship docks, passenger terminals, and services.

Walking distance to downtown Juneau, shops, and restaurants.

Key Border Crossings

Alcan Border (Tok)

Location: On the Alaska Highway (Route 2) near Tok, connecting Alaska with the Yukon Territory in Canada.

Importance: The most popular land entry point for those driving into Alaska.

Facilities:
U.S. Customs and Border Protection station.
Basic amenities such as gas stations and motels in nearby Tok.

Dalton Cache (Haines)
Location: On Haines Highway (Route 7) near Haines, connecting Alaska with British Columbia, Canada.
Importance: A scenic entry point, especially for those traveling to or from the Yukon and northern British Columbia.
Facilities:
U.S. Customs and Border Protection station.
Limited amenities; nearest town is Haines.
Tips:
Check road conditions, as this highway can be challenging, especially in winter.
Enjoy the scenic drive and take time to explore Haines and its surroundings.

Poker Creek – Little Gold Creek Border Crossing

Location: On the Taylor Highway (Route 5) near Chicken, connecting Alaska with the Yukon Territory in Canada.

Importance: The northernmost international border crossing in North America.

Facilities:
U.S. Customs and Border Protection station.
Very limited amenities; nearest services are in Chicken or Dawson City, Yukon.

By understanding these major entry points and preparing accordingly, you can ensure a smooth and enjoyable start to your Alaskan adventure.

Transportation Choices: Navigating Alaska by air, sea, and land.

By Air

Commercial Flights

Key Airports:

Ted Stevens Anchorage International Airport (ANC): The busiest airport, with frequent flights from the continental U.S. and international destinations.

Fairbanks International Airport (FAI): Important for reaching interior Alaska.

Juneau International Airport (JNU): Main gateway to Southeast Alaska.

Domestic Flights: Regular flights connect major cities like Anchorage, Fairbanks, and Juneau.

Airlines: Alaska Airlines, Delta, United, and others.

Bush Planes

Purpose: Essential for reaching remote and rural areas not served by larger aircraft.

Operators: Companies like Ravn Alaska, Grant Aviation, and Wright Air Service.

Routes: Serve communities, lodges, and national parks.

By Sea
Ferries

Alaska Marine Highway System (AMHS):

Routes: Connects coastal communities from the Aleutian Islands to Southeast Alaska.

Cost: $50 $300 depending on route and cabin type.

Facilities: Cabins, dining areas, lounges, and viewing decks.

By Land

Rental Cars

Availability: Major cities and airports like Anchorage, Fairbanks, and Juneau.

Cost: $50-$150 per day, depending on vehicle type and season.

Alaska Railroad

Routes:

Denali Star: Anchorage to Fairbanks, passing through Denali National Park.

Coastal Classic: Anchorage to Seward, offering stunning coastal views.

Glacier Discovery: Anchorage to Whittier, with scenic stops along the way.

Cost: $70-$200 depending on route and class of service.

Facilities: Dining cars, observation decks, and comfortable seating.

Buses and Shuttles

Public Buses: Available in larger cities like Anchorage and Fairbanks.
Cost: $2 per ride or $5 for a day pass.
Private Shuttles: Operate between major destinations and attractions.
Cost: Varies, typically $30 $100 depending on the route.

RV Rentals

Availability: Anchorage, Fairbanks, and other major cities.
Cost: $100- $300 per day, depending on RV size and season.

Cycling and Walking

Biking: Rental services available in cities like Anchorage.
Cost: $20- $50 per day.
Walking: Explore cities and trails on foot.
Tips:

Gear: Wear appropriate clothing and gear for changing weather conditions.

Safety: Be cautious of wildlife and follow safety guidelines.

General Tips for Getting Around

Weather: Always check weather conditions before traveling, as it can change rapidly.

Local Knowledge: Use local resources and advice to plan your routes and activities.

Flexibility: Be prepared for delays or changes, especially when traveling in remote areas or during winter months.

By air, sea, or land, navigating Alaska offers a range of transportation options tailored to different needs and preferences. Plan ahead and choose the methods that best suit your itinerary and budget for a smooth and enjoyable Alaskan adventure.

Iconic Road Trips: Scenic drives and itineraries for road trippers.

Alaska's vast and varied landscapes offer some of the most breathtaking road trips in the world. From coastal highways to rugged mountain routes, here are some iconic road trips that showcase Alaska's natural beauty:

The Parks Highway (Anchorage to Fairbanks)

Distance: Approximately 360 miles (580 km)
Highlights:
   Anchorage: Start your journey in Alaska's largest city.
   Denali National Park: Home to North America's highest peak, Mount Denali. Enjoy stunning views, wildlife, and outdoor activities.
   Healy: A small town offering additional access to Denali National Park.
   Fairbanks: End your trip in Alaska's interior city, known for its Northern Lights viewing and hot springs.
 Scenic Spots:

Denali Viewpoint: Panoramic views of Mount Denali.

South Denali Overlook: Stunning vistas of the mountain range and surrounding wilderness.

Tips:

Book in Advance: Reserve accommodations and tours, especially in peak season.

Weather: Be prepared for changing conditions, especially in the higher elevations.

The Seward Highway (Anchorage to Seward)

Distance: Approximately 125 miles (200 km)

Highlights:

Anchorage: Begin your trip in the city.

Turnagain Arm: A scenic fjord with dramatic views and frequent sightings of beluga whales.

Girdwood: A charming town with access to Alyeska Resort and beautiful glaciers.

Seward: A coastal town known for its marine life, Kenai Fjords National Park, and cruise opportunities.

Scenic Spots:

Beluga Point: Great spot for whale watching.

Portage Glacier: Viewable from a turnout or via a short hike.

Exit Glacier: A short drive from Seward with accessible glacier views.

Tips:

Activities: Consider taking a wildlife or glacier cruise in Seward.

Season: Summer offers the best weather and daylight for sightseeing.

The Sterling Highway (Anchorage to Homer)

Distance: Approximately 150 miles (240 km)

Highlights:

Anchorage: Start your drive in the city.

Kenai Peninsula: Explore the picturesque towns and natural attractions.

Ninilchik: Known for its Russian heritage and fishing opportunities.

Homer: The "Halibut Fishing Capital of the World," famous for its scenic harbor and outdoor activities.

Scenic Spots:

Turnagain Arm: Features stunning fjord views.

Kenai River: Offers opportunities for fishing and wildlife viewing.

Homer Spit: A unique landform extending into Kachemak Bay with shops and restaurants.

Tips:

Fishing: Book a fishing charter in Homer for a memorable experience.

Weather: Be prepared for variable weather, especially in coastal areas.

The Glenn Highway (Anchorage to Tok)

Distance: Approximately 200 miles (320 km)

Highlights:

Anchorage: Your starting point.

Eklutna Lake: A picturesque lake with hiking and biking trails.

Matanuska Glacier: A stunning glacier with opportunities for guided tours and ice climbing.

Tok: A gateway to the Alaskan interior and the Yukon Territory.

Scenic Spots:

Eklutna Lake: Beautiful turquoise waters and mountain views.

Matanuska Glacier Viewpoint: Fantastic views of the glacier.

Tanana River: Offers scenic views as you approach Tok.

Tips:

Glacier Tours: Consider booking a guided tour for a closer look at the Matanuska Glacier.

Road Conditions: Check for road conditions and closures, especially in winter.

The Dalton Highway (Fairbanks to Deadhorse)

Distance: Approximately 414 miles (666 km)

Highlights:

Fairbanks: Start in the interior city.

North Pole: A whimsical town with holiday themed attractions.

Arctic Circle: Cross the Arctic Circle and enjoy unique northern landscapes.

Deadhorse: The northernmost point accessible by road, near Prudhoe Bay and the Arctic Ocean.

Scenic Spots:

Yukon River: Offers stunning river views.
Arctic Circle Sign: A key milestone on the highway.
Prudhoe Bay: Explore the northernmost town and its surrounding landscapes.
Tips:
Preparation: This remote highway requires careful preparation and a reliable vehicle.
Safety: Be aware of weather conditions and road conditions; carry emergency supplies.

The Klondike Highway (Skagway to Dawson City)
Distance: Approximately 370 miles (595 km)
Highlights:
Skagway: A historic town with Gold Rush heritage.
White Pass: Scenic mountain pass with stunning views.
Dawson City: A historic town in the Yukon with a rich Gold Rush history.
Scenic Spots:
White Pass Scenic Railway: Offers a historic and scenic train ride.

Bonanza Creek: Famous for its Gold Rush history and picturesque landscapes.

Tips:

Border Crossing: Ensure you have proper documentation for crossing into Canada.

Season: Summer is the best time to travel due to weather and road conditions.

These iconic road trips offer a chance to experience Alaska's diverse landscapes, from coastal fjords to rugged mountains, and provide opportunities for adventure, sightseeing, and exploration.

Chapter 4: Cities and Towns

Alaska's cities and towns, from Anchorage's bustling energy to Fairbanks' rustic charm and Juneau's coastal beauty, each offer unique experiences. Anchorage is the gateway with diverse amenities, Fairbanks is a hub for adventure and Northern Lights, and Juneau blends history with stunning natural vistas. Each spot is a gem in Alaska's vast landscape.

Anchorage: Urban charm meets wilderness.

Anchorage, Alaska's largest city, uniquely blends urban convenience with rugged wilderness. Here's a detailed look at what makes this city a compelling destination:

Urban Charm
Cultural Attractions:
Anchorage Museum at Rasmuson Center: A key cultural institution featuring exhibits on Alaska's history, art, and science, including indigenous culture and the Northern Lights.
Alaska Native Heritage Center: Offers an immersive experience into Alaska Native cultures with interactive exhibits, traditional dance performances, and storytelling.

Dining and Shopping:

Restaurants: From fresh seafood to international cuisine, Anchorage has a diverse food scene. Notable spots include Simon & Seafort's for seafood and the Moose's Tooth Pub & Pizzeria for casual dining.

Shopping: Explore local shops and boutiques, including the Anchorage Market & Festival and the 4th Avenue Marketplace, offering unique Alaskan crafts and souvenirs.

Parks and Recreation:

Tony Knowles Coastal Trail: A scenic 11 mile trail ideal for biking, walking, or running, offering stunning views of Cook Inlet and the surrounding mountains.

Kincaid Park: A large park with trails for hiking and biking, plus beautiful views of the forest and coastline.

Accommodations:

Hotels: Anchorage offers a range of accommodations from luxury hotels like the Hotel Captain Cook to more budget friendly options. Many provide easy access to both urban and natural attractions.

Wilderness Integration
Proximity to Natural Wonders:
Flattop Mountain: A popular hiking destination with a relatively short, steep trail leading to a summit with panoramic views of Anchorage and the surrounding area.

Turnagain Arm: A scenic drive just outside Anchorage, known for its dramatic fjord landscapes and the possibility of seeing beluga whales.

Outdoor Activities:
Wildlife Viewing: Anchorage's nearby wilderness areas provide opportunities to see moose, bears, and other wildlife. Areas like the Anchorage Coastal Wildlife Refuge are prime spots for viewing.

Fishing and Kayaking: The city's lakes and rivers, such as Ship Creek, are excellent for fishing, while the waters of Cook Inlet offer kayaking and other water sports.

Winter Sports:

Skiing and Snowboarding: Alyeska Resort, located about an hour's drive from Anchorage, offers excellent skiing and snowboarding opportunities.

Snowshoeing and CrossCountry Skiing: Local parks like Kincaid and Hillside offer well maintained trails for winter sports enthusiasts.

Anchorage perfectly balances urban living with access to the wild beauty of Alaska. Its vibrant cultural scene, combined with its proximity to spectacular natural landscapes, makes it a unique gateway to both city life and wilderness adventure.

Juneau: Capital city with a smalltown feel.

Juneau, the capital of Alaska, combines the charm of a small town with the functions of a state capital. Here's a detailed look at what makes Juneau unique:

SmallTown Charm
Downtown Atmosphere:
Walkable Streets: Juneau's compact downtown area is easily navigable on foot, with charming streets lined with locally owned shops, restaurants, and historic buildings.

Historic District: Explore landmarks like the State Capitol Building, the Governor's Mansion, and the historic Red Dog Saloon, which has been serving patrons since 189

Local Dining and Shopping:
Restaurants: Enjoy fresh seafood and local cuisine at establishments like Tracy's King Crab Shack and The Hangar on the Wharf, which offer both excellent food and stunning waterfront views.

Shops: Browse local boutiques and art galleries for unique Alaskan crafts, jewelry, and souvenirs. The Alaska State Museum Store and other local shops feature items made by local artisans.

Community Events:

Local Festivals: Juneau hosts various events like the Juneau International Folklife Festival and the Alaska Folk Festival, celebrating local culture and traditions.

Farmers Markets: The Juneau Farmers Market offers fresh produce, local crafts, and baked goods, reflecting the town's community spirit.

Cultural Institutions:

Alaska State Museum: Offers in depth exhibits on Alaska's history, cultures, and natural environment, including indigenous art and artifacts.

JuneauDouglas City Museum: Focuses on the history of the area, including its gold rush past and early settlement.

Public Services:

Libraries and Community Centers: Juneau's libraries and community centers provide educational and recreational resources for residents and visitors alike.

Healthcare Facilities: As the regional hub for healthcare, Juneau has several medical facilities and services.

Access to Nature

Juneau's blend of small town charm and capital city amenities creates a unique and inviting atmosphere. Whether you're exploring its historic sites, enjoying local food and shopping, or venturing into the surrounding wilderness, Juneau offers a memorable Alaskan experience.

Fairbanks: Gateway to the Arctic and northern lights.

Fairbanks, situated in the heart of Alaska's interior, is renowned as the gateway to the Arctic and a premier destination for witnessing the Northern Lights. Here's a detailed look at what makes Fairbanks special:

Gateway to the Arctic
 Proximity to Arctic Circle:

Arctic Circle Tours: Fairbanks serves as a starting point for tours to the Arctic Circle. These tours often include scenic drives, wildlife viewing, and the opportunity to stand at the Arctic Circle sign.

TransAlaska Pipeline: The pipeline, which runs from the Arctic to Valdez, is accessible from Fairbanks. Visit the pipeline viewing area to learn about its engineering and significance.

Northern Exposure:

Explore the Wilderness: Fairbanks is a gateway to vast wilderness areas, including Denali National Park and the Yukon Territory. Outdoor enthusiasts can enjoy hiking, camping, and wildlife viewing in these remote regions.

Arctic Wildlife: Opportunities to see arctic animals such as caribou, musk oxen, and polar bears in their natural habitats.

Northern Lights Viewing
Aurora Borealis:

Optimal Viewing: Fairbanks is one of the best places in the world to view the Northern

Lights due to its location under the auroral oval. The lights are visible from late August to April.

Viewing Spots: Popular locations include the Chena Hot Springs Resort, where you can relax in natural hot springs while watching the aurora, and the Murphy Dome for panoramic views.

Local Attractions and Activities

Historical and Cultural Sites:

Museum of the North: Located at the University of Alaska Fairbanks, this museum offers exhibits on Alaskan art, history, and natural sciences, including indigenous cultures and the northern lights.

Pioneer Park: A historical park featuring museums, historic buildings, and cultural exhibits showcasing Fairbanks' gold rush history.

Accommodation:

Options: Fairbanks offers a range of accommodations from luxury lodges to budget hotels. Consider staying at places that offer aurora wakeup calls if you're visiting for the Northern Lights.

Local Insights:

Community: Engage with local residents and tour guides for insider tips on the best times and spots to see the Northern Lights and experience local culture.

Fairbanks combines its role as a gateway to the Arctic with stunning natural phenomena like the Northern Lights, offering visitors a unique blend of adventure, cultural experiences, and breathtaking natural beauty.

Smaller Gems: Highlighting quaint towns and hidden villages.

Alaska's charm extends beyond its well known cities. The state is dotted with quaint towns and hidden villages that offer unique experiences and a glimpse into local life. Here's a detailed look at some of these smaller gems:

Talkeetna

Location: Situated about 115 miles north of Anchorage, near the base of Denali.

Highlights:

Historic Downtown: Talkeetna's downtown is listed on the National Register of Historic Places, featuring rustic buildings, charming shops, and cozy cafes.

Denali Views: On clear days, you can see breathtaking views of Denali from the town.

Activities: Popular for flightseeing tours over Denali, river rafting on the Talkeetna and Susitna Rivers, and hiking.

Events: Known for quirky events like the Moose Dropping Festival and the Talkeetna Bluegrass Festival.

Haines

Location: Located in the northern part of the Alaska Panhandle, accessible by road, ferry, or small plane.

Highlights:

Wildlife Viewing: Known for the Chilkat Bald Eagle Preserve, which hosts one of the largest gatherings of bald eagles in the world.

Cultural Sites: The Sheldon Museum and Cultural Center and the Haines Native American Heritage Center provide insights into local history and indigenous culture.

Outdoor Activities: Hiking in the nearby mountains, fishing, and kayaking.

Festivals: Haines is home to the Southeast Alaska State Fair and the Great Alaska Craft Beer and Homebrew Festival.

Seward

Location: Located on the Kenai Peninsula, approximately 120 miles south of Anchorage.

Highlights:

Kenai Fjords National Park: Offers stunning glacial landscapes, abundant wildlife, and boat tours to see tidewater glaciers and marine life.

Alaska SeaLife Center: An important marine research facility and aquarium where you can learn about local marine life.

Historic Waterfront: Stroll along the waterfront with its murals, shops, and eateries.

Outdoor Activities: Hiking the Harding Icefield Trail, fishing, and exploring the Exit Glacier.

Petersburg

Location: Situated on Mitkof Island in the Alaska Panhandle, accessible by ferry or plane.
Highlights:
Norwegian Heritage: Known as "Little Norway," Petersburg celebrates its Norwegian roots with traditional architecture and festivals.

Fishing Community: A working fishing town where you can observe fishing boats and explore seafood markets.

Wildlife and Nature: Excellent opportunities for wildlife viewing, including whales, seals, and sea birds. The nearby LeConte Glacier is a popular destination.

Festivals: Hosts the annual Little Norway Festival celebrating Norwegian Constitution Day.

Wrangell

Location: Located on Wrangell Island in the Alaska Panhandle, accessible by ferry or plane.

Highlights:

Historical Sites: Visit the Wrangell Museum and Chief Shakes Tribal House to learn about the town's history and Tlingit heritage.

Petroglyph Beach: A unique beach featuring ancient rock carvings.

Outdoor Activities: Fishing, kayaking, and hiking. The Anan Wildlife Observatory offers one of the best places to see bears in their natural habitat.

Festivals: The Wrangell Bearfest celebrates bears and their role in the ecosystem.

Homer

Location: Situated on the Kenai Peninsula, known as the "Halibut Fishing Capital of the World."

Highlights:

Homer Spit: A narrow landform with shops, restaurants, and opportunities for fishing and wildlife tours.

Art and Culture: Home to many artists, with numerous galleries and the Pratt Museum showcasing local art and history.

Kachemak Bay: Offers kayaking, wildlife viewing, and beautiful scenery. Take a water taxi to explore nearby Halibut Cove.

Outdoor Activities: Fishing, hiking, and exploring the many trails and parks in the area.

These smaller gems provide a more intimate and authentic Alaskan experience, allowing you to immerse yourself in the state's natural beauty and cultural richness away from the larger, more touristy cities.

Chapter 5: Nature and Wildlife

Alaska's nature and wildlife are unparalleled, offering breathtaking landscapes and incredible wildlife encounters. From towering glaciers and dense forests to diverse fauna like bears, moose, and whales, the state is a haven for nature lovers.

Every visit promises aweinspiring beauty and unforgettable experiences in the great outdoors.

National Parks and Preserves: Exploring Denali, Glacier Bay, and more.

Alaska's national parks and preserves offer some of the most stunning and diverse landscapes in the world. Here's an indepth look at some of the most notable parks:

☐ **Denali National Park and Preserve**
Overview:
    Location: Interior Alaska, north of Anchorage.
    Size: Over 6 million acres, centered around North America's highest peak, Denali (formerly Mount McKinley).

Key Attractions:
    Denali: Standing at 20,310 feet, it's a major draw for mountaineers and sightseers.
    Wildlife: Home to the "Big Five" – grizzly bears, wolves, caribou, moose, and Dall sheep.

Visitors can also see eagles, foxes, and numerous bird species.

Activities:
Bus Tours: The park road is primarily accessible via parkoperated buses, offering narrated tours with wildlife spotting and stunning vistas.

Hiking: Trails range from easy walks near the visitor center to challenging backcountry routes.

Wildlife Viewing: Best done early in the morning or late in the evening.

☐ Visitor Centers:

Denali Visitor Center: Offers exhibits, films, and rangerled programs.

Eielson Visitor Center: Provides panoramic views of Denali and interpretive displays.

Glacier Bay National Park and Preserve
Overview:

Location: Southeast Alaska, part of the Inside Passage.

Size: Over 3 million acres, encompassing tidewater glaciers, rugged mountains, and deep fjords.

Key Attractions:

Glaciers: Tidewater glaciers like Margerie and Johns Hopkins are constantly calving, creating spectacular sights and sounds.

Marine Life: Waters teeming with humpback whales, orcas, sea lions, seals, and sea otters. Birdwatchers can spot puffins, eagles, and many seabirds.

Activities:

Boat Tours: The primary way to explore the park, offering closeup views of glaciers and wildlife.

Kayaking: Provides an intimate experience with the park's waterways and wildlife.

Hiking: Trails range from easy walks to more strenuous routes through temperate rainforests and along shorelines.

☐ **Visitor Centers:**
Glacier Bay Visitor Center: Located in Bartlett Cove, offers exhibits, a bookstore, and rangerled programs.
Lodge and Campground: Accommodations and dining options available for extended stays.

Katmai National Park and Preserve
Overview:
Location: Southwest Alaska, on the Alaska Peninsula.
Size: Over 4 million acres, known for its volcanic landscapes and abundant brown bears.

Key Attractions:
Brooks Falls: Famous for bear viewing, especially during the salmon runs in July and September.
Valley of Ten Thousand Smokes: A dramatic volcanic landscape formed by the 1912 eruption of Novarupta.

Activities:

Bear Viewing: Platforms at Brooks Falls offer safe, closeup viewing of bears fishing for salmon.

Fishing: Worldclass sport fishing for salmon and trout.

Hiking: Trails through diverse landscapes, from lush forests to volcanic valleys.

☐ Visitor Centers:

Brooks Camp Visitor Center: Provides information on the park's natural and cultural history, along with bear safety guidelines.

Kenai Fjords National Park
Overview:

Location: Southcentral Alaska, near the town of Seward.

Size: Over 600,000 acres, featuring a mix of glaciers, fjords, and marine life.

Key Attractions:

Harding Icefield: One of the largest icefields in the United States, feeding over 40 glaciers.

Wildlife: Common sightings include puffins, sea otters, humpback whales, and orcas.

Activities:

Boat Tours: Explore the fjords and see calving glaciers, marine wildlife, and dramatic coastal scenery.

Hiking: The Harding Icefield Trail offers a challenging but rewarding hike with spectacular views.

Kayaking: Paddle through calm waters, explore hidden coves, and encounter marine life.

Visitor Centers:

Kenai Fjords Visitor Center: Located in Seward, offers exhibits, films, and ranger programs.

Exit Glacier Nature Center: Provides information and trails to view Exit Glacier up close.

❖ **WrangellSt. Elias National Park and Preserve**

Overview:

Location: Southeast Alaska, near the Canadian border.

Size: Largest national park in the U.S., encompassing over 13 million acres.

Key Attractions:

Mountain Ranges: Home to nine of the 16 highest peaks in the U.S., including Mount St. Elias.

Glaciers and Rivers: Massive glaciers and braided river systems dominate the landscape.

Activities:

Hiking and Mountaineering: Extensive trails and challenging climbs for experienced adventurers.

Wildlife Viewing: Bears, moose, caribou, and mountain goats are common sightings.

Flightseeing: A popular way to experience the park's vast and rugged terrain.

☐ Visitor Centers:

WrangellSt. Elias Visitor Center: Located in Copper Center, offers exhibits and rangerled programs.

Kennecott Mines National Historic Landmark: Provides a glimpse into the region's mining history.

Alaska's national parks and preserves offer unparalleled opportunities to experience the state's natural beauty and wildlife. Each park has its own unique features and attractions, providing diverse and memorable adventures for visitors.

Wildlife Encounters: Where to see bears, eagles, whales, and other iconic species.

Alaska is renowned for its rich and diverse wildlife. Here are some of the best places and tips for encountering iconic Alaskan species:

Bears

Brooks Falls, Katmai National Park:

Highlights: Famous for its large population of brown bears, especially during the salmon runs in July and September. The viewing platforms provide safe, closeup encounters.

Activities: Guided bear viewing tours, photography opportunities, and educational programs.

Admiralty Island National Monument:

Highlights: Known as the "Fortress of the Bears," this area has one of the highest brown bear densities in the world.

Activities: Bear viewing at Pack Creek Bear Viewing Area, where you can watch bears fishing for salmon.

Anan Wildlife Observatory, Wrangell:

Highlights: Offers viewing of both black and brown bears as they fish for salmon in Anan Creek.

Activities: Guided tours and safe viewing platforms.

Eagles

Chilkat Bald Eagle Preserve, Haines:
Highlights: Home to the largest concentration of bald eagles in the world, especially during the late fall and winter.
Activities: Guided eaglewatching tours, educational programs, and photography opportunities.

Kodiak Island:
Highlights: Abundant eagle population, often seen perched in trees or soaring above the coast.
Activities: Birdwatching tours, kayaking, and hiking along the coast.

Kenai Peninsula:
Highlights: Common sightings of bald eagles, particularly around the Kenai River and coastal areas.

Activities: Scenic drives, river rafting, and guided wildlife tours.

Whales

Glacier Bay National Park:

Highlights: Known for humpback whales, especially during the summer months. Orcas, gray whales, and minke whales can also be spotted.

Activities: Boat tours, kayaking, and rangerled programs.

Seward and Resurrection Bay:

Highlights: Popular for humpback and orca sightings. You may also see gray whales during their migration periods.

Activities: Whalewatching cruises, kayaking, and coastal hikes.

Juneau:

Highlights: A prime location for whale watching, with frequent sightings of humpback whales and orcas.

Activities: Whalewatching tours, kayaking, and photography excursions.

Alaska's diverse ecosystems provide unique and plentiful opportunities to see a wide range of iconic wildlife species in their natural habitats, offering unforgettable experiences for nature lovers and wildlife enthusiasts.

Outdoor Activities: Hiking, kayaking, and adventure sports in the wild.

Alaska is a paradise for outdoor enthusiasts, offering a vast array of activities amidst its breathtaking landscapes. Here's an indepth look at some of the best outdoor activities:

Hiking
Harding Icefield Trail, Kenai Fjords National Park:
  Difficulty: Strenuous
  Highlights: This 2mile roundtrip trail offers stunning views of Exit Glacier and the expansive Harding Icefield. The trail passes through lush forests, alpine meadows, and rocky outcrops.

Tips: Bring layers for changing weather conditions, and start early to allow plenty of time for the hike.

Flattop Mountain, Anchorage:
Difficulty: Moderate to difficult
Highlights: One of the most popular hikes in Anchorage, this 3mile roundtrip trail provides panoramic views of the city, Cook Inlet, and the surrounding mountains.
Tips: The final ascent involves some scrambling over rocks, so be prepared for a bit of a challenge.

Mount Healy Overlook Trail, Denali National Park:
Difficulty: Moderate
Highlights: This 5mile roundtrip trail offers spectacular views of the Alaska Range and the Nenana River valley. The trail climbs steadily through spruce forest to a rocky outcrop.
Tips: Look out for wildlife along the trail, including Dall sheep and caribou.

Root Glacier Trail, WrangellSt. Elias National Park:
Difficulty: Moderate
Highlights: This 4mile roundtrip trail takes you to the edge of the Root Glacier, where you can explore ice formations and crevasses. Guided ice climbing and glacier hiking tours are available.
Tips: Wear sturdy boots and consider hiring a guide for a safe glacier experience.

Kayaking
Prince William Sound:
Highlights: Paddle through calm, protected waters surrounded by towering mountains, glaciers, and dense forests. Wildlife sightings may include sea otters, seals, and orcas.
Popular Routes: Blackstone Bay, Columbia Glacier, and Harriman Fjord.
Tips: Guided tours are recommended for beginners. Dress in layers and bring waterproof gear.

Kenai Fjords National Park:

Highlights: Kayak among icebergs and tidewater glaciers, with opportunities to see marine wildlife such as sea lions, puffins, and humpback whales.

Popular Routes: Aialik Bay, Northwestern Lagoon, and Holgate Arm.

Tips: Weather can change quickly, so be prepared with appropriate gear. Consider a guided tour for safety and local knowledge.

Kachemak Bay, Homer:

Highlights: Explore the rich marine ecosystem, with chances to see sea otters, bald eagles, and harbor seals. The bay offers protected waters and stunning coastal scenery.

Popular Routes: Halibut Cove, Grewingk Glacier Lake, and Peterson Bay.

Tips: Tides can be significant, so plan your trip accordingly. Kayak rentals and guided tours are available in Homer.

Adventure Sports

Whitewater Rafting:

Six Mile Creek, Kenai Peninsula:

Difficulty: Class IVV rapids

Highlights: Thrilling rapids, steep drops, and narrow canyons make this one of the most exciting whitewater experiences in Alaska.

Tips: Suitable for experienced rafters. Outfitters provide necessary gear and safety briefings.

Nenana River, Denali National Park:

Difficulty: Class IIIV rapids

Highlights: Scenic river with stunning views of Denali and the Alaska Range. Raft through canyons and past glacialfed waters.

Tips: Various sections cater to different skill levels. Guided tours are available for all experience levels.

Ice Climbing:

Root Glacier, WrangellSt. Elias National Park:

Highlights: Experience the thrill of climbing blue ice formations and exploring deep crevasses on this accessible glacier.

Tips: Guided tours provide equipment and training. Suitable for beginners and experienced climbers.

Matanuska Glacier, near Anchorage:
Highlights: A popular spot for ice climbing and glacier trekking, with stunning ice formations and accessible routes.

Tips: Several outfitters offer guided climbs and provide necessary equipment.

Backcountry Skiing and Snowboarding:
Chugach Mountains, near Valdez:

Highlights: Worldclass powder and challenging terrain attract expert skiers and snowboarders. Helicopter and snowcat skiing provide access to remote areas.

Tips: Suitable for advanced skiers. Guides and safety equipment are highly recommended.

Turnagain Pass, Chugach National Forest:
Highlights: Easily accessible backcountry terrain with deep snow and stunning views. Popular for both skiing and snowboarding.

Tips: Avalanche awareness and proper safety gear are essential. Check conditions and consider a guided tour for safety.

Alaska's diverse landscapes and pristine wilderness provide endless opportunities for outdoor adventure, from serene kayaking trips to adrenalinepumping whitewater rafting and challenging hikes.

Chapter 6: Unique Alaskan Experiences

Alaska offers truly unique experiences, from witnessing the stunning northern lights and exploring vast glaciers to participating in the Iditarod dog sled race and visiting remote indigenous villages. These adventures immerse you in the state's rich culture and breathtaking natural beauty, creating memories that last a lifetime.

Glacier Adventures: Cruise, hike, and fly over stunning ice formations.

Experiencing Alaska's glaciers is like stepping into a different world—one of immense ice fields, towering blue seracs, and the raw, powerful beauty of nature. Here's how you can immerse yourself in these breathtaking landscapes:

☐ **Glacier Cruises**

Kenai Fjords National Park:

Highlights: Cruise through the park's fjords to see tidewater glaciers like Aialik and Holgate, where you might witness dramatic calving events as massive chunks of ice break off into the sea.

Wildlife: Spot humpback whales, orcas, sea lions, puffins, and sea otters along the way.

Experience: These cruises often include narration by knowledgeable guides who provide insights into the geology and ecology of the region.

Glacier Bay National Park:
Highlights: Embark on a journey through Glacier Bay, home to more than 50 named glaciers. Marvel at the sheer size and beauty of Margerie and Johns Hopkins glaciers.

Wildlife: Keep an eye out for marine life such as seals, porpoises, and a variety of seabirds.

Experience: Cruises often feature park rangers on board who share the history and significance of the area.

Prince William Sound:
Highlights: This area offers spectacular glacier cruises, with Columbia Glacier being a standout. The glacier's face is constantly changing, providing an everevolving spectacle.

Wildlife: Encounter otters, seals, and perhaps even a black bear along the shoreline.

Experience: The serene waters and stunning ice formations create a tranquil yet aweinspiring adventure.

☐ **Glacier Hiking**
Exit Glacier, Kenai Fjords National Park:
Highlights: Accessible by road, Exit Glacier offers a range of hiking options. The Edge of the Glacier Trail allows you to get up close to the ice, while the Harding Icefield Trail provides panoramic views.

Experience: Walk through lush forests and alpine meadows before reaching the glacier's edge, where you can feel the cool breeze off the ice and hear the creaks and groans of the glacier moving.

Matanuska Glacier:
Highlights: As one of the most accessible glaciers in Alaska, you can drive up to the glacier and explore it on foot.

Experience: Guided tours take you across the glacier's surface, where you can peer into deep blue crevasses and touch ancient ice. The knowledgeable guides share fascinating details about the glacier's history and dynamics.

Root Glacier, WrangellSt. Elias National Park:

Highlights: This lessvisited gem offers a more intimate glacier hiking experience. The trail to the glacier passes through beautiful landscapes before reaching the ice.

Experience: Don crampons and hike across the glacier's surface, exploring ice caves and moulins (deep, vertical shafts). The quiet, remote setting enhances the sense of adventure and discovery.

☐ Glacier Flightseeing
Denali National Park:

Highlights: Take to the skies for a bird'seye view of Denali's vast glaciers, including the massive Kahiltna Glacier. Flights often circle North America's highest peak, offering unparalleled views.

Experience: The sheer scale of the glaciers and the mountain landscape from above is breathtaking. Some tours even offer glacier landings, allowing you to step out onto the ice.

Juneau Icefield:

Highlights: Helicopter tours from Juneau provide stunning views of the icefield's many glaciers, including the famous Mendenhall Glacier.

Experience: Land on the glacier and experience its icy expanse firsthand. Many tours include guided walks on the ice, where you can explore ice formations and learn about the glacier's features.

Ruth Glacier, Denali National Park:

Highlights: Known as the Great Gorge, Ruth Glacier is one of the deepest in the world, with ice up to 3,800 feet thick. Flightseeing tours offer a closeup view of this impressive natural wonder.

Experience: Flying through the Great Gorge, with its towering granite walls and vast ice field, is a surreal experience. The pilot's commentary enhances your understanding of this majestic landscape.

Exploring Alaska's glaciers by cruise, hike, or flight offers unforgettable adventures, allowing you to experience the aweinspiring power and beauty of these natural wonders up close.

Dog Sledding: Embrace the spirit of the Iditarod.

Dog sledding in Alaska is more than just a thrilling winter activity—it's a deep dive into the state's rich history and culture. The Iditarod, known as "The Last Great Race on Earth," epitomizes the spirit of endurance, teamwork, and adventure that dog sledding embodies. Here's how you can experience it:

☐ The Iditarod Trail

Historical Significance:

Origins: The Iditarod Trail began as a mail and supply route in the early 20th century, connecting remote communities and gold mining camps. It gained fame in 1925 during the "Great Race of Mercy" when sled teams delivered diphtheria serum to Nome, saving many lives.

The Race Today: The Iditarod Trail Sled Dog Race, established in 1973, commemorates this heroic journey. Mushers and their teams cover over 1,000 miles from Anchorage to Nome, braving extreme weather and rugged terrain.

☐ **Experiencing Dog Sledding**
Winter Dog Sledding:

Mushing Tours: Many tour operators offer dog sledding experiences where you can ride in the sled or even learn to mush your own team. Popular locations include Fairbanks, Anchorage, and Denali National Park.

Day Trips and MultiDay Expeditions: Options range from short rides to multiday expeditions, where you can camp out in the wilderness and learn more about sled dog care and handling.

Best Time: The prime season for dog sledding is from November to April, with peak conditions in February and March.

Summer Dog Sledding:

Glacier Dog Sledding: During the summer months, helicopter tours from places like Juneau, Seward, and Girdwood take you to snowcovered glaciers where you can experience dog sledding in a spectacular setting.

Dryland Mushing: Some kennels offer dryland mushing experiences, where sleds on wheels are used. This is a great way to enjoy dog sledding without snow.

☐ **Learning from the Experts**
Kennel Tours:

Meet the Dogs: Visit kennels where you can meet the dogs, learn about their training, and see how they are cared for. Kennel tours are available in many parts of Alaska, including Willow, home to many Iditarod mushers.

Interactive Demonstrations: Many kennels offer demonstrations and handson experiences, giving you a taste of what it takes to prepare for and run in a race.

Mushing Schools:

Training Programs: For those who want a more immersive experience, some schools offer intensive training programs where you can learn the skills needed to mush your own team.

Workshops and Clinics: These are great for beginners and provide a comprehensive introduction to the sport, covering everything from harnessing dogs to steering a sled.

☐ The Iditarod Experience

Watching the Race:

Anchorage Start: The ceremonial start in downtown Anchorage is a festive event, with spectators cheering on mushers as they embark on their epic journey.

Willow Restart: The official restart in Willow offers another opportunity to see the teams up close and witness the excitement as they head into the wilderness.

Following the Race: Throughout March, you can follow the race online, tracking mushers' progress and watching live updates from checkpoints.

Participating in Iditarod Events:

Meet the Mushers: Leading up to the race, events like the Musher Banquet in Anchorage offer a chance to meet mushers and hear their stories.

Volunteer Opportunities: For a more handson experience, consider volunteering at the race. Volunteers help with everything from checkpoint operations to dog care.

Embracing the Spirit of the Iditarod

Dog sledding in Alaska is an unforgettable experience that connects you with the state's rugged wilderness and its storied past. Whether you're gliding across snowy landscapes in winter or mushing on a glacier in summer, the thrill of dog sledding and the bond with these incredible dogs will leave you with lasting memories and a deep appreciation for the spirit of the Iditarod.

Aurora Borealis: Best practices for chasing the northern lights.

Witnessing the Aurora Borealis, or northern lights, is a bucketlist experience for many travelers. Alaska, with its clear skies and minimal light pollution, offers some of the best opportunities to see this natural wonder. Here's a guide to help you maximize your chances of experiencing the mesmerizing dance of the northern lights.

☐ **When to Go**
Optimal Season:

Winter Months: The best time to see the northern lights in Alaska is from late August to early April. The peak months are typically September and March, when solar activity is highest, and nights are long and dark.

Time of Night:

Late Night to Early Morning: The auroras are most active between 10 PM and 2 AM. However, they can be seen as early as 7 PM and as late as 6 AM, so staying up late or waking up early increases your chances.

☐ **Where to Go**
Fairbanks:
Why Fairbanks: Located under the "Auroral Oval," Fairbanks is one of the best places in the world to see the northern lights. It offers numerous viewing spots and tours.

Viewing Spots: Chena Hot Springs, Cleary Summit, and Murphy Dome are popular spots for clear, unobstructed views.

Denali National Park:
Why Denali: With its vast, dark skies, Denali provides excellent aurora viewing opportunities, especially in the winter months when the park sees fewer visitors.

Viewing Spots: Anywhere with a clear, northern horizon within the park is ideal.

Brooks Range:

Why Brooks Range: For a more remote and adventurous experience, the Brooks Range offers pristine viewing conditions with minimal light pollution.

Viewing Spots: Gates of the Arctic National Park and Anaktuvuk Pass.

Chasing the northern lights in Alaska is a magical experience that requires a bit of planning and patience. By choosing the right time and place, checking forecasts, dressing warmly, and being prepared for photography, you can greatly increase your chances of witnessing and capturing this incredible natural phenomenon. Whether you go it alone or join a guided tour, the sight of the aurora borealis dancing across the Alaskan sky is an unforgettable adventure.

Chapter 7: Historical and Cultural Sites

Alaska's historical and cultural sites, like the Klondike Gold Rush National Historical Park and Sitka National Historical Park, offer a rich mosaic of Indigenous heritage and early American history. Explore Native art, gold rush tales, and WWII history, revealing Alaska's diverse and dynamic past.

Native Heritage: Visiting cultural centers and learning about indigenous history.

Exploring Native Heritage in Alaska offers a profound understanding of the region's Indigenous peoples. Visiting cultural centers like the Alaska Native Heritage Center in Anchorage or the Sitka National Historical Park provides immersive experiences into the rich traditions, art, and history of Alaska's Native communities. These centers often feature exhibits on traditional crafts, storytelling, and historical artifacts, allowing visitors to engage directly with Indigenous cultures.

Educational programs and guided tours can shed light on historical events, such as the impacts of colonization and the resilience of Native communities. Additionally, participating in cultural workshops, such as drummaking or weaving, helps visitors appreciate the craftsmanship and significance behind Indigenous practices. Engaging with local Indigenous guides and attending community events further enhances the experience, offering personal insights and fostering a deeper respect for Alaska's Native heritage.

Gold Rush Legacy: Tracing the steps of fortune seekers.

Tracing the Gold Rush Legacy in Alaska transports visitors to the era of the Klondike Gold Rush, a pivotal moment that shaped the region's history. Sites like the Klondike Gold Rush National Historical Park in Skagway and Dawson City offer authentic glimpses into the lives of fortune seekers who flocked to Alaska in the late 19th century.

Visitors can explore preserved mining camps, historical buildings, and engaging exhibits that recount the challenges and triumphs of the gold rush era. Walking along the same trails as the prospectors, such as the Chilkoot and White Pass trails, provides a tangible connection to the arduous journey they undertook. Interactive exhibits and reenactments at these sites vividly illustrate the rush for gold and its impact on Alaska's development.

The legacy of the gold rush is also visible in the boomtown architecture, mining equipment, and stories of those who risked everything for fortune. By tracing these historical footsteps, visitors gain insight into the dramatic transformations and enduring spirit that defined Alaska during this transformative period.

Museums and Historic Landmarks: Preserving Alaska's storied past.

Museums and historic landmarks in Alaska play a crucial role in preserving and interpreting the state's rich and diverse history. Key institutions include:

Alaska State Museum: Located in Juneau, this museum showcases extensive collections of Native Alaskan artifacts, historical documents, and art. Exhibits cover a broad spectrum, from indigenous cultures and early exploration to modern Alaskan life, offering a comprehensive view of the state's heritage.

Anchorage Museum at Rasmuson Center: This museum combines science, history, and art, featuring exhibits on Alaska's natural history, indigenous cultures, and the impact of exploration. Its handson exhibits and multimedia presentations make it an engaging destination for all ages.

Sitka National Historical Park: This site preserves the Tlingit culture and the historical conflict with Russian explorers. Visitors can explore the totem poles, historical Russian structures, and the RussianAmerican Company cemetery, gaining insight into the area's cultural and historical significance.

Klondike Gold Rush National Historical Park: This park in Skagway preserves the history of the Klondike Gold Rush. Visitors can explore restored buildings, historical artifacts, and take part in rangerled tours that detail the hardships and adventures of the gold rush era.

These museums and landmarks not only preserve artifacts and stories but also offer interactive and educational experiences, ensuring that Alaska's multifaceted history is accessible and engaging for both residents and visitors.

Chapter 8: Culinary Delights

Alaska's culinary scene offers a unique blend of flavors influenced by its diverse landscape and rich cultural heritage. Key highlights include:

Fresh Seafood: Alaska is renowned for its seafood, with fresh catches like king crab, salmon, halibut, and shellfish taking center stage. Local favorites include salmon smoked or grilled, and crab served in various styles, from crab cakes to hearty crab legs.

Wild Game: Game meats such as caribou, moose, and venison are staples in Alaskan cuisine. These meats are often featured in hearty stews, roasts, and sausages, reflecting the state's hunting traditions and rustic culinary style.

Foraged Ingredients: Alaskan chefs often incorporate foraged ingredients like wild berries, mushrooms, and seaweed into their dishes. Local berries, such as lingonberries and crowberries, are used in jams, desserts, and sauces, adding unique flavors to the cuisine.

Native Alaskan Cuisine: Indigenous dishes reflect traditional methods and local ingredients. Options include dishes like akutaq (Eskimo ice cream), which blends berries, animal fat, and sugar, and various traditional soups and stews.

Craft Beverages: Alaska boasts a growing craft beverage scene with local breweries producing unique beers, often using local ingredients like spruce tips and berries. Additionally, local distilleries create spirits like vodka and gin, crafted from Alaskan grains and botanicals.

Dining in Alaska provides an opportunity to experience the state's rich natural bounty and culinary creativity, with many restaurants and markets celebrating local ingredients and traditional recipes.

Local Flavors: Signature dishes and regional specialties.

Alaska's local flavors are a testament to its diverse landscape and rich cultural history. Signature dishes and regional specialties include:

King Crab: Known for its sweet, succulent meat, King Crab is a celebrated delicacy in Alaska. Often served steamed or boiled, it's a highlight of seafood menus, sometimes accompanied by melted butter or garlic sauce.

Salmon: Alaska's wild salmon is renowned for its quality and flavor. Popular preparations include smoked salmon, grilled salmon fillets, and salmon chowder. Variants like sockeye and king salmon are particularly prized.

Halibut: This versatile white fish is often breaded and fried, served as fish and chips, or prepared as a grilled steak. Its mild flavor and firm texture make it a favorite in various culinary styles.

Reindeer Sausage: Also known as caribou sausage, this specialty is a staple at many Alaskan eateries. It's often served in sandwiches, as a breakfast item, or as part of a charcuterie board.

Akutaq: Often referred to as Eskimo ice cream, akutaq is a traditional Alaskan dessert made from berries, animal fat (such as caribou or seal), and sweeteners. It's a unique blend of indigenous ingredients and flavors.

Baked Goods: Alaskan bakeries offer treats that often incorporate local ingredients, such as berry pies (blueberry, lingonberry), sourdough pancakes, and dense rye bread.

Seafood Stews and Chowders: Hearty stews and chowders featuring a mix of seafood, potatoes, and vegetables are common in Alaskan cuisine. These dishes are comforting and reflect the state's reliance on fresh, local ingredients.

These signature dishes highlight Alaska's rich culinary heritage, offering a taste of the state's natural bounty and cultural influences.

<u>Dining Recommendations: From gourmet restaurants to cozy diners.</u>

Alaska offers a diverse dining scene, ranging from highend gourmet establishments to charming, cozy diners. Here are some recommendations across the spectrum:

☐ Gourmet Restaurants:

Nina's (Anchorage): Known for its upscale dining experience, Nina's offers a refined menu with a focus on fresh, local seafood and game meats. The ambiance is elegant, making it perfect for a special occasion.

The Crow's Nest (Anchorage): Located on the top floor of the Hotel Captain Cook, The Crow's Nest provides stunning panoramic views and a sophisticated menu featuring Alaskan seafood, steaks, and a comprehensive wine list.

Kincaid Grill (Anchorage): This restaurant blends gourmet dining with a relaxed atmosphere, serving up a mix of contemporary and classic dishes with an emphasis on local ingredients, including fresh seafood and wild game.

☐ Cozy Diners:

Snow City Café (Anchorage): A beloved local spot known for its hearty breakfasts and brunches. Popular dishes include stuffed French toast, crab omelets, and a variety of baked goods.

The Silver Gulch Brewing and Bottling Co. (Fox): Located near Fairbanks, this brewpub offers a cozy atmosphere with a selection of craft beers brewed onsite. Their menu features comfort foods like burgers, sandwiches, and hearty stews.

The Alaska Coffee Roasting Co. (Anchorage): A perfect spot for coffee lovers, this café serves locally roasted coffee and a selection of pastries and light bites. It's a great place to relax and enjoy a casual meal.

49th State Brewing Company (Anchorage): A popular choice for both locals and visitors, this brewery offers a relaxed setting with a menu featuring hearty pub fare, craft beers, and unique Alaskan dishes like reindeer sausage.

Additional Suggestions:
The Rustic Goat (Anchorage): **Offers a casual atmosphere with a focus on farmtotable dishes, including locally sourced meats and vegetables.**

Tanana Valley Café (Fairbanks): **Known for its friendly service and homey atmosphere, this café serves up classic diner fare with a local twist.**

These dining spots provide a range of experiences, whether you're looking for an elegant night out or a casual, comforting meal.

Brewery and Distillery Tours: Tasting the best of Alaska's craft beers and spirits.

Alaska's craft beer and spirits scene is vibrant and varied, offering unique flavors inspired by the state's natural bounty. Here are some top recommendations for brewery and distillery tours:

☐ Brewery Tours:
Alaska Brewing Company (Juneau):
Tour Highlights: Explore one of Alaska's most established breweries, known for its flagship beer, Alaskan Amber. The tour covers the brewing process and includes tastings of a range of beers.
Specialties: Alaskan Amber, White Ale, and seasonal brews like the Alaskan Smoked Porter.

Midnight Sun Brewing Co. (Anchorage):
Tour Highlights: This brewery is known for its innovative beers. Tours offer a

behindthescenes look at their brewing process and provide tastings of their unique creations.

Specialties: Arctic Rhino IPA, Sockeye Red Pale Ale, and their seasonal brews.

49th State Brewing Company (Anchorage):
Tour Highlights: Enjoy a tour that showcases the brewery's approach to crafting beers using local ingredients. The tour often includes a tasting session.

Specialties: 49th State Pale Ale, Birchwood Brown Ale, and a rotating selection of seasonal beers.

Silver Gulch Brewing and Bottling Co. (Fox):
Tour Highlights: Located near Fairbanks, this brewery offers tours that delve into their brewing techniques and the history of the brewery, with tastings of their craft beers.

Specialties: Silver Gulch IPA, Arctic Amber, and their seasonal selections.

☐ Distillery Tours:
Anchorage Distillery (Anchorage):

Tour Highlights: This distillery focuses on producing highquality spirits with a local twist. The tour provides insight into their distillation process and includes tastings of their spirits.

Specialties: Alaska Vodka, Alaskan Gin, and specialty infusions.

Willow Distillery (Willow):

Tour Highlights: Known for its handcrafted spirits and unique flavors, Willow Distillery offers tours that highlight their production process and the story behind their spirits.

Specialties: Willow Distillery's flagship vodka and seasonal liqueurs.

Matanuska Distillery (Palmer):

Tour Highlights: Enjoy a tour of this smallbatch distillery that emphasizes locally sourced ingredients and traditional methods. Tastings include their range of crafted spirits.

Specialties: Matanuska Alaska Vodka and specialty liqueurs.

Boreal Spirits (Anchorage):

Tour Highlights: Boreal Spirits focuses on using Alaskan botanicals in their products. Their tours highlight the use of local ingredients and the unique aspects of their distillation process.

Specialties: Boreal Gin and Alpenglow Liqueur.

These tours offer a great opportunity to taste and learn about Alaska's diverse craft beers and spirits, each with its own unique story and flavor profile.

Chapter 9: Accommodation Options

Alaska's accommodation options range from luxury lodges with stunning views and topnotch amenities to cozy cabins and budgetfriendly motels. Whether you seek an upscale retreat in the wilderness or a charming stay in town, there's something for every traveler's taste and budget.

Luxury Lodges and Resorts: Indulgent stays in breathtaking settings.

Luxury lodges and resorts in Alaska offer an unparalleled experience, blending indulgent comfort with breathtaking natural beauty. These accommodations are designed to provide a high level of service and exclusivity, making them perfect for a luxurious getaway.

Notable Luxury Lodges and Resorts:
Tutka Bay Lodge (Kachemak Bay):
Features: Accessible only by boat or floatplane, Tutka Bay Lodge provides an intimate, allinclusive experience. It offers luxurious waterfront cabins with stunning views of the bay and surrounding wilderness. The lodge specializes in personalized adventure packages, including wildlife viewing, fishing, and kayaking.

Highlights: Gourmet dining featuring local ingredients, guided excursions, and a serene, remote location.

The Alyeska Resort (Girdwood):
Features: Located in the picturesque town of Girdwood, The Alyeska Resort is Alaska's largest ski resort, offering elegant accommodations with panoramic views of the surrounding mountains and Turnagain Arm. It features a worldclass spa, fine dining, and access to a range of outdoor activities.

Highlights: Skiin/skiout access, luxury spa treatments, and gourmet dining with views.

Hotel Captain Cook (Anchorage):
Features: This upscale hotel in Anchorage provides refined accommodations with sweeping views of the city and surrounding mountains. It offers luxurious rooms, a fullservice spa, and a variety of dining options. Its central location is ideal for exploring Anchorage.

Highlights: Elegant rooms, comprehensive amenities, and fine dining options.

Land's End Resort (Homer):
Features: Perched on a peninsula, Land's End Resort offers luxurious accommodations with views of Kachemak Bay and the Kenai Mountains. Guests can enjoy upscale rooms and suites, a spa, and fine dining while watching the tides and wildlife.

Highlights: Beautiful coastal views, gourmet restaurant, and proximity to outdoor adventures.

Borealis Basecamp (Near Fairbanks):
Features: This unique luxury camp offers a chance to experience the Northern Lights in style. Guests stay in domed glass igloos that provide unobstructed views of the aurora borealis. The camp combines modern comforts with an immersive natural experience.

Highlights: Northern Lights viewing, cozy igloo accommodations, and a unique glamping experience.

Staying in one of these luxury lodges or resorts provides not just a place to stay, but a complete experience where comfort and natural beauty converge, offering an unforgettable Alaskan adventure.

MidRange Hotels and Inns: Comfort and convenience for every traveler.

Midrange hotels and inns in Alaska strike a balance between comfort, convenience, and affordability, offering travelers a reliable and enjoyable stay.

Notable MidRange Hotels and Inns:

Puffin Inn (Anchorage):

Features: Located conveniently near Anchorage's airport and downtown, Puffin Inn offers comfortable rooms with modern amenities. Guests can enjoy complimentary breakfast, free WiFi, and a range of room options.

Highlights: Proximity to the airport, free breakfast, and comfortable accommodations.

Hotel Alyeska (Girdwood):

Features: While slightly higher in range, Hotel Alyeska provides a midrange option with upscale touches. It features cozy rooms, a spa, and easy access to the Alyeska Ski Resort. The hotel offers a mix of comfort and luxury in a beautiful setting.

Highlights: Skiin/skiout access, stunning views, and onsite dining.

SpringHill Suites by Marriott (Anchorage):

Features: This hotel offers spacious suites with separate living areas, ideal for families or longer stays. Guests benefit from a fullservice business center, a fitness room, and a complimentary breakfast.

Highlights: Spacious suites, free breakfast, and convenient location.

Homer Inn & Spa (Homer):

Features: Located near the waterfront in Homer, this inn offers a relaxing atmosphere with ocean views. It features comfortable rooms, a spa, and easy access to local dining and activities.

Highlights: Ocean views, spa services, and proximity to local attractions.

Best Western Plus Pioneer Park Inn (Fairbanks):
Features: This hotel combines comfort and convenience with wellappointed rooms, an indoor pool, and a complimentary breakfast. It is located near Fairbanks' main attractions and offers good value for money.
Highlights: Indoor pool, complimentary breakfast, and central location.

Midrange hotels and inns are a great choice for travelers seeking a comfortable and convenient stay while exploring Alaska, offering a range of amenities and a welcoming atmosphere without breaking the bank.

Chapter 10: Travel Tips and Safety

Traveling to Alaska presents unique opportunities and challenges. Here are some essential travel tips and safety advice to ensure a smooth and enjoyable experience:

❖ **Travel Tips:**
Pack Layers: Alaska's weather can be unpredictable, so bring layers to adjust to varying temperatures. Include waterproof and windproof outerwear, especially if you're venturing into outdoor activities.

Plan for Daylight Variations: Depending on the time of year, daylight hours can vary dramatically. In summer, you might experience nearly 24 hours of daylight, while winter brings long nights. Plan your activities accordingly.

Book in Advance: Accommodations and tours can fill up quickly, especially during peak tourist seasons. Book lodging and activities well in advance to secure your preferred options.

Prepare for Outdoor Activities: If you're engaging in outdoor adventures like hiking, fishing, or wildlife viewing, ensure you have the appropriate gear and understand the local conditions. Check for permits or regulations required for certain activities.

Be Wildlife Aware: Alaska is home to diverse wildlife, including bears and moose. Learn about wildlife safety and carry bear spray if you're hiking or camping. Maintain a safe distance from all wildlife.

Stay Hydrated and Eat Well: The dry air and altitude can be dehydrating. Drink plenty of water and maintain a balanced diet to keep your energy levels up.

Check Road Conditions: If you're driving, especially on rural roads, check for current road conditions and weather forecasts. Some roads may be closed or impassable due to weather or construction.

- ❖ **Safety Tips:**

Emergency Contacts: Familiarize yourself with local emergency services and the nearest medical facilities. Have contact numbers for local authorities and emergency services readily available.

Travel Insurance: Consider purchasing travel insurance that covers medical emergencies, trip cancellations, and lost luggage. It's particularly useful for trips involving outdoor activities.

Health Precautions: Alaska has a low risk of disease, but it's still wise to follow general health precautions. Ensure you're up to date on routine vaccinations and consult with your healthcare provider before traveling.

Follow Local Guidelines: Adhere to local guidelines and regulations, particularly regarding wildlife interactions and environmental conservation. Respect signs and barriers, especially in natural parks and reserves.

By following these travel tips and safety guidelines, you can make the most of your Alaskan adventure while ensuring your wellbeing and security throughout your trip.

Weather and Safety Precautions: Staying safe in diverse climates and terrains.

Alaska's diverse climates and terrains require careful planning to stay safe while traveling. Here are some key weather and safety precautions to consider:

☐ **Weather Precautions:**
Layer Your Clothing: Alaska's weather can vary greatly within a single day. Wear layers that can be added or removed as conditions change. Include moisturewicking base layers, insulating midlayers, and waterproof outer layers.

Check Weather Forecasts: Regularly check local weather forecasts, especially if you're planning outdoor activities. Be aware of conditions like fog, rain, snow, or extreme temperatures that could impact your plans.

Prepare for Temperature Extremes: Depending on the season and location, temperatures can range from mild to freezing. In winter, ensure you have adequate insulation and protection against frostbite, including gloves, hats, and thermal socks.

Sun Protection: In summer, especially during extended daylight hours, wear sunscreen, sunglasses, and a hat to protect against sunburn and glare, even if temperatures are cooler.

Snow and Ice Safety: If traveling in snowy or icy conditions, ensure your vehicle is equipped with snow tires or chains. Be cautious of slippery sidewalks and trails; use traction devices if needed.

☐ **Terrain Precautions:**

Know Your Route: Familiarize yourself with your route, whether it's hiking, driving, or exploring. Research trail conditions, road closures, and potential hazards.

Carry Navigation Tools: Use GPS devices, maps, or trail apps to navigate, particularly in remote areas where cell service might be unreliable. Ensure your devices are fully charged.

Stay on Marked Trails: When hiking, stick to established trails to avoid getting lost and to minimize your impact on the environment. Be aware of trail markers and follow them.

Prepare for Altitude: If traveling to higher elevations, acclimate slowly to avoid altitude sickness. Drink plenty of water and avoid strenuous activity until you adjust.

Wildlife Awareness: Understand wildlife behavior and safety protocols. Keep a safe distance from animals, and carry bear spray in bear country. Store food properly to avoid attracting wildlife to your campsite.

By following these weather and safety precautions, you can navigate Alaska's diverse climates and terrains with greater confidence and ensure a safe and enjoyable trip.

Respecting Wildlife and Nature: Guidelines for responsible tourism.

Respecting wildlife and nature is crucial for responsible tourism, especially in a pristine and sensitive environment like Alaska. Here are key guidelines to ensure you're minimizing your impact and enjoying nature responsibly:

☐ **Wildlife Safety and Respect**

Keep a Safe Distance: Always observe wildlife from a safe distance. Do not approach, feed, or disturb animals. Use binoculars or a zoom lens to view them without getting too close.

Follow Wildlife Viewing Guidelines: Adhere to specific guidelines provided by parks, tour operators, or wildlife organizations. These guidelines are designed to protect both wildlife and visitors.

Bear Safety: In bear country, make noise while hiking to avoid surprising bears. Carry bear spray and know how to use it. Store food securely and use bearproof containers or hanging systems.

Respect Breeding Seasons: During certain times of the year, wildlife may be more sensitive due to breeding or nesting. Avoid disturbing nests, dens, or areas with young animals.

Avoid Feeding Animals: Feeding wildlife disrupts their natural behavior and can lead to dependency on human food. It can also attract animals to human areas, creating potential hazards.

Emergency Contacts and Resources: Essential information for peace of mind.

Having access to emergency contacts and resources is crucial for a safe and enjoyable trip to Alaska. Here's a guide to essential information for peace of mind:

Emergency Contacts:

Emergency Services (Police, Fire, Medical):

Phone Number: *911*

Note: This number is universally used for emergency situations requiring immediate response, such as medical emergencies, fires, or crimes.

Local Medical Facilities:

Anchorage: Providence Alaska Medical Center – *+1 9075622211*

Fairbanks: Fairbanks Memorial Hospital – *+1 9074565454*

Juneau: Bartlett Regional Hospital – *+1 9077968900*

Note: Find the nearest hospital or urgent care center based on your location.

Search and Rescue (SAR):

Phone Number: Contact local authorities or the Alaska State Troopers for SAR assistance.

Note: For situations requiring rescue, especially in remote areas.

☐ **Resources:**

Travel Insurance Providers:

Note: Ensure you have travel insurance that covers medical emergencies, trip cancellations, and other unforeseen events. Contact your provider for assistance in case of an emergency.

☐ **Local Visitor Information Centers:**

Anchorage: Anchorage Visitor Information Center – *+1 9072791500*

Fairbanks: Fairbanks Convention & Visitors Bureau – *+1 9074565774*

Juneau: Juneau Convention and Visitors Bureau – *+1 9075862201*

Note: These centers can provide local advice, directions, and emergency assistance.

☐ **National Park Service (NPS) – Alaska:**

Phone Number: *+1 9076443500*

Website: [nps.gov/ak](https://www.nps.gov/ak)

Note: For information on national parks, safety tips, and regulations.

☐ **Alaska Department of Transportation (DOT):**

Phone Number: *+1 9074653900*
Website: dot.alaska.gov
Note: For road conditions, closures, and transportationrelated emergencies.

☐ **Local Weather Services:**
Website: [weather.gov/anc](https://www.weather.gov/anc) (Anchorage)
Website: [weather.gov/fairbanks](https://www.weather.gov/fairbanks) (Fairbanks)
Note: For current weather conditions and forecasts.

Wildlife Safety:
Phone Number: Contact local wildlife agencies or the Alaska Department of Fish and Game for advice on dealing with wildlife encounters.
Website: [adfg.alaska.gov](http://www.adfg.alaska.gov)

Additional Tips:

Save Contact Information: Store emergency contacts and important numbers in your phone and have a physical copy in your travel documents.

Local Resources: Know the location of the nearest police station, hospital, and visitor information center relative to where you're staying.

Cell Service: Be aware that cell service can be limited in remote areas. Consider renting a satellite phone if traveling to isolated locations.

Having these emergency contacts and resources at your disposal ensures you're wellprepared for any unforeseen situations, allowing for a safer and more enjoyable Alaskan adventure.

Final thoughts

Traveling to Alaska offers an incredible opportunity to experience some of the most stunning landscapes and unique wildlife in the world. Here are a few final thoughts to keep in mind:

Embrace the Adventure:

Explore Widely: Alaska's vastness and diversity offer a range of experiences, from icy glaciers and rugged mountains to vibrant wildlife and rich cultural history. Take the time to explore various regions and activities to fully appreciate what the state has to offer.

Be Prepared: Given Alaska's unpredictable weather and remote locations, preparation is key. Pack appropriately for various conditions, and stay informed about local weather and travel advisories.

Respect the Environment:

Follow Guidelines: Adhere to guidelines for wildlife safety and environmental conservation to help preserve Alaska's pristine beauty. Respect local customs and natural habitats to ensure a positive impact.

Leave No Trace: Practice responsible tourism by minimizing your environmental footprint. Follow the "Leave No Trace" principles and respect the natural surroundings.

Stay Safe:
Know Your Resources: Keep essential contact information and emergency resources handy. Familiarize yourself with local services and safety protocols to handle any unexpected situations.

Travel Smart: Consider travel insurance and be aware of local regulations and safety tips. Whether you're hiking in the backcountry or exploring a city, staying informed and prepared will enhance your safety.

Cherish the Experience:
Capture Memories: Alaska's landscapes are breathtaking and offer unique photo opportunities. Capture your experiences and take

the time to reflect on the beauty and adventure you've encountered.

Share the Joy: Whether through stories, photos, or recommendations, sharing your experiences can inspire others to explore and appreciate Alaska's wonders.

With thoughtful planning and respect for the environment, your trip to Alaska can be a memorable and enriching experience. Enjoy the adventure and the stunning natural beauty that makes Alaska truly special.

Printed in Great Britain
by Amazon